ROSEMARY CLINCH

BOSSINEY BOOKS

First published in 1987
by Bossiney Books,
St Teath, Bodmin, Cornwall

All Rights Reserved
© 1987 Rosemary Clinch
ISBN 0 948158 29 8

Typeset, printed and bound by
WBC Print Ltd, Bristol

Acknowledgments

The author would like to give especial thanks to Portmeirion Ltd for their kind assistance, Jack Minnitt, Sun Life Assurance Archivist, for his continued interest and Mrs Peter Heath for her generosity. Photographs have been supplied as follows: David Mansfield (front cover), George Gallop, Mildred Ford, Portmeirion Ltd, Mrs Peter Heath, Brunel University Library, SS Great Britain Project, Arts Faculty Photographic Unit, University of Bristol, Rosemary and Michael Clinch.

About the Author and the Book

Rosemary Clinch, who lives at Littleton-on-Severn, completes a Bristol double for Bossiney. In 1985 she wrote *Unknown Bristol*, a book which has gone rapidly into reprint. David Foot, in his perceptive Introduction, reflected: 'I get the firm impression that Rosemary Clinch relishes looking round the corners and under the pavement stones just like I do.'

It is this curiosity and intuitive quality which makes her the natural author for *Curious Bristol*. Of the earlier Bristol title, *The Book Exchange* referred to her skill in 'getting into the nooks and crannies of Bristol', and another reviewer likened her approach to that of the great James Cameron, the journalist who looked *beyond* the facts.

Rosemary has also contributed a section on presentday characters in *People and Places in Bristol*, introduced by bestselling novelist E. V. Thompson.

'To be curious is to have the spirit of adventure, to turn a dull world into a treasure house of exciting discoveries' is how she opens this, her latest book. She then proceeds to investigate 'that curious "something" which has made Bristol a place of great achievement.' Characters and curious corners, streets and eerie tales which defy human explanations are only some of the subjects of this fascinating journey around a city which has often led London and the rest of the country. Photographs, ancient and modern, combine to capture the spirit of the place.

In addition to her books on Bristol, Rosemary Clinch is the author of *Supernatural in Somerset*, a chapter in *Strange Somerset Stories*, and co-author of *Unknown Somerset*, *Secret Westcountry* and *King Arthur in Somerset*.

Of her exploration among the Arthurian sites, publisher Michael Williams has written: 'Like that great Westcountry traveller and writer, Lady Clara Vyvyan, Rosemary has the ability to captivate both the eye and the mind . . . she is a real Arthurian student — a seeker par excellence.'

To my husband Michael for his encouragement

Contents

Curious Bristol

'Stay curyous Traveller and pass not bye . . .'
T. Chatterton 1768

To be curious is to have the spirit of adventure, to turn a dull world into a treasure house of exciting discoveries. Curiosity is powerful.

It beckoned the great explorers, many of whom sailed from Bristol, eager to learn of what lay westward over the great horizon. Men like Cabot, Martin Pring and Admiral William Penn, who, as John Harvey said, 'were pioneers of a vast expansion which was to make their language the most widely spoken upon the face of the earth'.

It is that curious 'something' which has made Bristol a place of great achievement, a city leading London and the rest of the country in a string of impressive 'firsts'. Among them, the first workhouse, established by Act of Parliament, the first savings bank, the first free library, the first American Consulate and the first Methodist chapel in the world.

Bristol made the first English brass and produced porcelain from clay. It saw the first steamship planned and built in its docks, was a major influence in the Great Western Railway project and became the birthplace for supersonic flight. McAdam revolutionised the roads from Bristol, and many remarkable men and women parade the pages of Bristol's history — Edward Colston, philanthropist and founder of schools, Dr W. G. Grace, the creator of modern cricket, Samuel Plimsoll, dubbed 'the sailors' friend' because of his famous Plimsoll

Right: 'The Spirit of Bristol representing and capturing within its steel form the city's traditional feeling of energy and enterprise.'

SHELDON BUSH & PATENT SHOT CO

Above: Strange shapes decorate the futuristic lines of a city. In the courtyard of the Sun Life building, in St James Barton, 'Monolith II' by John Maine may puzzle some, but it integrates beautifully with the company's symbol. The carved forms in white Carrara marble trap the sunlight and cast a continuous movement of shadows throughout the day, while the yellow-grey walls of the courtyard act as a foil.

Left: The Shot Tower rising above the floating harbour.

Above: Thunderbolt Steps — a steep climb to Totterdown from the Bath Road.

Right: The Everard Building in Broad Street.

line, Hannah More, writer and social worker, George Muller, pastor and founder of Bristol orphanages, the poets Chatterton and Southey are only some of them. More recently Bristol has nurtured that great military commander Field Marshal Viscount Slim and film star Cary Grant.

This intrinsic element is at the very heart of Bristol. Hard to grasp, it has been 1000 years in the making. From the beginning Bristol has succeeded, its prosperity, independence and beautiful architecture drawing the curious to visit the second most important city in the country. Somehow Bristolians found the courage and strength to rebuild after the strife of war and depression, while preserving and

GUTENBURG
MORRIS
EDWARD
EVERARD

safeguarding what was left of their great heritage. Today this element, this enterprising spirit, has extended old boundaries. Its influence is shaping the city of the future, yet, in this age of technology and leisure, aspects from past centuries blend with the natural scenery and urban industry.

Although curiosity can be dissipated by familiarity, Bristol is still proud of its famous and unusual sights which continue to attract the visitor. Two familiar landmarks are the leaning tower of Temple Church and the shot tower. Behind busy Victoria Street, the ruins of Temple Church have been preserved since the second world war but it came as a surprise to those dealing with bomb damage that the tower had not been affected by the devastation; it had been leaning since the fourteenth century. A curious legend has it that the tower was built on a foundation of wool packs in an area of thriving cloth workers. The land was marshy and the foundations insecure, so during the first stage of building the tower subsided to one side. Before the upper two sections were added it was strengthened by underpinning, leaving it firm but leaning nearly five feet out of alignment.

The shot tower in Cheese Lane, not far from Temple Church, stands in complete contrast overlooking the floating harbour. Its straight clean lines rise to a twelve-sided barrel-shaped room, where molten lead when poured through a perforated plate falls into water below, solidifying into spherical shot. This marvel of invention was due to the curiosity of an eighteenth-century Redcliffe plumber, William Watts, who found his inspiration in a strange dream.

Bristol is rich in curious things to whet the appetite. To be seen by every passer-by is the Everard building in Broad Street, a brave touch of Art Nouveau, sitting amid the traditional walls of history. Built as a printing house in 1900 for Edward Everard, the exotically coloured and preserved façade, in Carrara marble-ware tiles, depicts literary and angelic figures with an alphabet. It may shock or delight but it can invoke a sense of fun.

At Clifton's Goldney House, private except on special occasions, is its fascinating Grotto, a whimsey of the rich, decorated with thousands of shells and quartz known as 'Bristol diamonds'. Like several of Bristol's wealthy men, Thomas Goldney, a Quaker grocer,

Right: St Mary Redcliffe Church: 'A place of spiritual refreshment and artistic beauty.'

added his own particular brand of creation to enhance the already beautiful surroundings to his house.

The origins of street names remain curious mysteries, like *Christmas* in Christmas Steps and Street, while *There and Back Again Lane* behind Georges Bookshop in Park Street is self-explanatory as it is a cul-de-sac. Unfortunately it encourages the less acceptable face of curiosity for periodically the sign disappears, prompting the thought that, perhaps, today a more fitting name would be *There and Gone Again Lane.*

The unique character of Bristol presents a landscape, towered and turreted, over a warren of alleyways, cobbled streets and waterways. It has fascinated people for centuries while the countless villages absorbed among its urban sprawl provide still more discoveries. There is the charm of the unexpected, and great variety to arouse the curiosity: the splendours of places of worship, period buildings, artistic statues and the relics of museums; Bristol's green oases; the many quiet corners of the past; the bustling streets; and even the occupations of its people. Whether an item for respect or a matter for mirth, the need to know more can be a joy, opening windows on the past and adding colour to the present.

Right: Into the author's possession came this fascinating study from the 1800s. A proud owner of a 'penny-farthing' designed by James Starley but could the owner of the 'boneshaker' possibly be Bristolian?

What is it?

Below: Near Bristol Bridge in High Street, an impression of ancient Egypt surrounds this door, but the steps inside lead down to a fine example of one of Bristol's medieval cellars.

Right: It may seem out of place to visitors at St Mary Redcliffe Church but there it remains in the churchyard, a reminder of wartime. A massive bomb explosion sent this piece of tram rail flying through the air from the Redcliffe Hill area to land as we see it today in the turf.

Left: No, it is not a vandalised post box in Colston Avenue! It is really a rather splendid access point to the underground River Frome.

Above: In Leonard Lane the walls of the old city are long gone, but an old Parish marker remains. It is still possible to trace a line of the ancient wall through St Nicholas Street, High Street and Tower Lane to St John's Arch.

Up, Along and Under

When the Montgolfier brothers burned straw and wool beneath a huge silk bag in France in 1783, the astonished crowd saw it leave the earth little realising they had witnessed man's first conquest of the air. It was not long before Bristol, too, saw balloons lift off and land. In 1784, one of the first to be seen in England came down in St George. The place is still known today as Air Balloon Hill. Balloon mania had arrived, even 'landing', for keen collectors, on all manner of articles from crockery and glassware to head-dresses and clocks.

In a field behind Stokes Croft, in 1810, thousands gathered to watch the beginning of the celebrated flight of England's first aeronaut, James Sadler, and William Clayfield of Clifton. They saw the largest and most beautiful balloon of all rise gracefully into the air, but the voyage was not to be without incident. After launching near Ashton Court a cat in a basket equipped with a parachute, they drifted across the Channel to Cardiff where they drank the health of 'Colonel Gore and the Bristol Volunteers' and Mr Sadler lost his hat. Changing course, they arrived at Bideford, then Barnstaple, where they drank to 'Absent Friends'. Needing more height, they frantically 'ditched' a great-coat, a barometer, a speaking-trumpet and the grappling iron! When the gas finally gave out they came down in the sea to be rescued by a boat from Lynmouth, but the brave men had covered the best part of 100 miles.

While an obsession to fly persisted, a curious invention early in the nineteenth century gave another meaning to 'go fly a kite' for those

Left: In St Nicholas Street the mysterious veiled face of a lady looks down from no. 18. The architects of the building, although well-known, left no record of her significance.

Overleaf: Balloon mania at Ashton Court in 1986.

travelling on *terra firma*. Aeropleustic science, George Pocock, a Bristol schoolmaster, called it, as he effectively 'severed' the horse from the carriage, attached some kites and renamed it the 'Charvolant'. Sceptical onlookers watched in amazement a horseless carriage full of people being pulled along in a brisk wind at up to 25 miles per hour. 'Those who travel by kites, travel as Kings,' he said and was eventually commanded to show his invention to George IV. But it did not catch on even though its design absolved people from paying heavy turnpike tolls.

In 1836, when the foundation stone of Clifton Suspension Bridge was laid, George Pocock sent up five very large balloons. Attached to one was a streamer saying 'success to the undertaking'. Neither Pocock nor Brunel would ever have guessed at the curious feats to come from future aeronauts whose comment on the bridge would be 'it wants flying under'.

Air Chief Marshal Sir Dermot A. Boyle once said of those who reach for the skies that they 'display traditional British virtues — love of adventure, endurance in adversity and an irrepressible sense of humour'. He was probably well aware that for some high spirited RAF pilots, bravery could easily turn to bravado. Those 'daring young men in their flying machines' would 'lose their goggles' or go 'loopy', as my father would say, while he *never* risked his beloved Hawker Fury — or so he said.

Flying under Clifton Suspension Bridge seems to have been a temptation for pilots almost since aeroplanes first flew. 'It just *asks* to be flown under,' said Group Captain Peter Heath when he related an extraordinary history of daring flights before he died in 1984. Having served with No. 25 Squadron, he would have been well aware of the amazing manoeuvrability of the Hawker Fury, an aeroplane which thrilled the public with aerobatic displays at Hendon in the late 1930s.

He also found, through personal research in later years, that

Left: Group Captain Peter Heath. 'It just asks to be flown under!'

buf-puf
Toys
FESTO
ELECTRONIC
G-BBOC

BALLOO
Schroder
Life
Imperial
TYPEWRITERS

Clifton's bridge had encouraged an impromptu kind of aerobatic fever since 1911. 'It seems the first pilot to give way to temptation was a Frenchman, M. Tetard, smartly followed in 1912 by someone once reported as Alan Cobham, mistakenly I think,' related Peter. 'Somebody certainly went through in 1912 because the police stopped an Englishman having a shot the next year, when a ban was imposed on the whole idea because of danger to people below or damage to the bridge itself. Possible damage to the pilot does not seem to have come into it.

'That ban did not survive long into the first world war. By 1916 there was a flying training unit, No. 66 Squadron, at Filton and those pilots were soon 'eyeing' the bridge. One evening in the Mess, Lieutenant Basil Scott-Foxwell announced that he might have a go and accepted a bet from his instructor for five pounds — a lot of money in those days. So on Christmas morning, 1916, the two set off in separate aircraft, Scott-Foxwell to go through the bridge while his instructor stayed up aloft to "see that he damn well did". And he did, flying along above the Gorge from Avonmouth and dipping under the bridge at the last moment. Scott-Foxwell did not enjoy it much and thought it a hard-won fiver. Not surprising really, with the unreliability of the little 80–100 h.p. rotary engine in the old Avro with a top speed of about 80 m.p.h. The flight must have been the first, I think, of that era because they became so frequent later that no-one would have wagered five bob, let alone five pounds on it.'

Peter went on to say that witnesses were actually on the bridge as aircraft flew under them, while others saw the amazing sight of formations of three going through usually 'on Sunday afternoons after Sunday School at Clifton'. He gained some fascinating evidence from a Mr Downs who, as a youth, worked in the top terminus of the Rocks Railway near the Vincent Rocks Hotel. 'The hotel usually had about a dozen pupil pilots billeted in it and they all knew Arthur Downs. They would tip him off. "Watch tomorrow morning, Arthur." He would and, as he put it, "Someone would always go through the bridge, two or three times a week sometimes." Probably by that time, no self respecting pupil thought himself fully fledged unless he had "done the bridge". Reprehensible possibly, but when you remember that, once they got to France, their life-expectancy was statistically just three weeks, you can hardly blame them. A Lieutenant P.G. Taylor went through in those days but a Pilot Officer K.T. Irwin and a Squadron Leader Shales both claimed to

The Hawker Fury which 'thrilled the public with aerobatic displays.'

have "looped the bridge". Shales, I understand, did it later in 1920, long after leaving Filton when he would have been flying Bristol Fighters, much more powerful machines. I have flown them myself and, yes, they loop very nicely — but sooner him than me.'

When the war ended the Gorge and Bridge were also left in peace. Then in 1930 a Mrs Hunt saw, from the Portway, a small aeroplane 'dip gently under the bridge and climb quietly away. No fuss, no noise.' The description fitted that of a civilian D.H. Moth. Three months later on a September morning, 'a Siskin fighter went clattering through, flipped up over Leigh Woods and vanished'. Peace reigned once again. The second war, unlike the first, saw stricter controls over aircraft, their services fulfilling a more desperate need.

During this time Clifton College was used as a Headquarters for the 1st American Army and they kept a few small aircraft on The Close. Maybe our gum-chewing friends were 'bitten by the bug' as

Clifton Suspension Bridge. A misty day on the Portway — not the weather for flying under bridges.

what was probably an Auster took a 'jolly' under the bridge in 1943 and 1945. Then in the autumn of 1945, at over twice the speed of the Auster, Lieutenant Dennis Hartas, RNAS flew across from Yeovilton in a Corsair to put on a show for a favourite Aunt (Christmas coming up?). He finished his display doing 300 knots and had to make such a steep turn into the Gorge that he thought he was going to hit the cliff by Sion Hill. The close-up he got of that cliff — and perhaps of Auntie as well — scared him stiff. However, he missed them both and went on for a long career with British Airways.

In 1955 RAF Weston Zoyland grounded its Meteors to investigate which culprit, if any, had at the time flown under the bridge. The more powerful the aircraft obviously the more expertise required to fly them and this love of adventure which resulted in such escapades needed tempering. As Peter related, not everyone survived the curious call of the bridge.

'The next and last flight under the bridge ended in tragedy. On Sunday, 3 February 1957, No. 501 (City of Bristol) Auxiliary Squadron was to hold a parade and fly-past to mark its final disbandment. Prior to this, in the morning, Flight Officer John Greenwood Crossley flight-tested his Vampire fighter and, presumably, to mark the occasion in a less official manner, shot through the bridge at what the current newspapers reported as "terrific speed". High speed was nearly the undoing of Lieutenant Hartas, and Crossley was flying probably half as fast again. Sadly, he misjudged things and hit the Gorge-side at Leigh Woods, killing himself instantly.

'After that, as far as I can discover, no-one else has tried. Times, aircraft and pilots have changed. The light-hearted pilot-boys of the wars, who would stick two fingers up at authority on the slightest provocation, have gone. The modern service aircraft is too fast, too heavy to flip casually in and out of gorges, and, perhaps, everything is taken a little more seriously now. You might say that the bridge, with its beautiful massive dignity, has seen them all off and won. It is for the best I suppose but, as a one-time wayward pilot-boy myself, I sometimes look at Clifton Suspension Bridge, shake my head slowly and think — Y'know. That thing still wants flying under!'

Characters

How right E.V. Thompson is when he says, in *People and Places in Bristol*, that the city 'has always had a great many men and women who might best be referred to as "unusual characters".' As a Bristol policeman he had a rare insight into many personalities especially the less fortunate who inhabit the streets, the neglected places, the hidden corners. He reminds me of others in the Force before him, showing compassion and understanding in the hard world of people like 'Paper Sally' who sold papers in central Bristol. When she tragically died in a fire in her paper-filled rooms on Christmas Day in 1926, the police of 'A' Division gave her a fitting funeral, a tribute for a well-loved character.

Looking further back into history, I find there were some characters who by their nature could be considered *very* curious and in some cases positively 'dotty'. The Quaker, James Nayler, chose the intolerant age of the 1650s to announce he was the Messiah and greatly incensed the people of Bristol. To make matters worse he gained a large following of admirers whose religious fervour openly displayed their belief that he was superhuman. Riding from Bedminster to Broad Street on the back of a donkey to cries of 'Hosanna' and the waving of branches was 'the last straw'. He was promptly hauled off to prison in London, branded on his cheek with a 'B' for blasphemy, a hole bored through his tongue and returned to Bristol for whipping through the streets. After further confinement in London, he returned, to live in Bristol, a much quieter man.

Another curious character who intrigued me was a distressed young lady who turned up at a house in Almondsbury in 1817. She spoke no English — just a kind of 'gibberish' which no-one could interpret. The house belonged to a local squire, Samuel Worall, who took her in and gave her work while trying to trace who she was. Her diet was strange, mostly vegetarian except for fish and pigeons' heads.

Paper Sally Bristol

Princess Caraboo came to Almondsbury.

She fasted on one day and prayed in eastern fashion. Eventually it was learned through a foreign visitor that she was a Princess Caraboo and had been abducted from the region of Sumatra and held by the captain of a ship until she escaped when it docked at Bristol. Sadly, it was all the stuff of dreams, for her inevitable popularity produced someone who actually knew her. In reality she was Mary Baker, a domestic servant and the daughter of a Bristol cobbler. Embarrassment caused her to be sent to America where for all we know she may have again played out her romantic dreams. Not so romantically she returned to Bedminster some years later, sold leeches to earn a living and died in 1864.

More puzzling than Princess Caraboo, although in some way similar, are the strange revelations of the 'Maid of the Haystack'. Described as 'of prepossessing appearance and graceful manners, but obviously of disordered intellect', she arrived at a house in Flax Bourton in 1776 asking for milk. Afterwards she explored the fields and found a haystack, under which she sheltered for several days, while women in the area took pity on her, supplying her with food and drink.

No one could persuade her to stay in a house until she became deranged and was removed to St Peter's Hospital in Bristol where she remained for a year or so. Her health restored, she immediately returned to the stackyard at Flax Bourton, preferring the haystack to the protection of a roof. Local gentry provided her food but were unable to find out who she was or where she came from. Despite having a peculiar accent, she only spoke English, but she did infer she had come from a family of some distinction.

Among the many people interested to see the 'Maid' was Hannah More who felt she would be better cared for in a lunatic asylum at Hanham, while attempts were made to establish her identity. A story called 'A Tale of Real Woe' was published in a London newspaper and various papers in France and Germany. Nothing resulted until in 1785 an anonymously written pamphlet in French entitled *The Unknown; a True Story* claimed to identify the 'Maid' as the half-sister of the Queen of France and natural daughter of the Emperor Francis I. The pamphlet alleged, although no proof was given, that a young lady living in style in Bordeaux in 1769 had gained the favours of dignitaries including the Duke of York. The Empress enraged at finding out the lady was the Emperor's daughter, had her arrested, carried off to Belgium and left at Ostend with £50 to fend for herself. The pamphlet became a bestseller with suspicions of it being the work of 'a masked libeller of the house of Austria'. Translated into English it made three editions and whether people believed the story or not, Hannah More did. She continued to care for the 'Maid' or Louisa, the name she was eventually given. As Louisa's mental condition worsened to helpless idiocy, Miss More removed her to a lunatic house attached to Guy's Hospital in London, contributing to her maintenance and paying for the expense of her funeral when she died in 1800. The mystery was never solved but some believed it was likely the 'Maid of the Haystack' was probably simply a gypsy who because of her derangement was driven from her tribe.

What on Earth . . . ?

Bristol can be full of surprises with sights curious enough to draw the crowds.

Above: The sound of jackboots in Welsh Back, but it is not an invasion from the past! Members of the cast prepare for a 'take' during the filming of a scene for the television production of *The Diary of Anne Frank*.

Above: Another day and a different age presents itself as the cry of 'stand and deliver' is heard in Newgate. Modern Bristol witnesses an older type of 'heist' staged by the Post Office. All part of the fun to advertise the opening of the Security '85 Exhibition held at the Holiday Inn.

Down in the harbour something stirs. Planks and rigging creak while the *Golden Hinde* visits Bristol before embarking on another voyage.

Things which go 'Bump' and Bite

When Odeon Cinema Manager, Mr Jackson, was shot dead while on duty in 1946, the murderer was never found and the case has remained unsolved. Some believe the spirit of Mr Jackson haunts the Odeon, while in the restaurant next door he is said to be responsible for dinner tables being stripped of menus and glasses.

'That's not all either,' said Rita Morgan, owner of the popular New Yorker restaurant. 'I have watched a "J" cloth being ripped in front of my eyes.' Rita seemed quite resigned to having 'spooky' visitations as she told me how curious things have been going on in the cinema and in her restaurant for a long time. 'I often heard doors banging in the cinema when working late into the early hours, but how do you explain why they went on banging when the place was gutted to a shell for refurbishment. It seemed to get worse then, so perhaps the changes upset him. Although things have been quieter recently, even a cleaner in the cinema told me she has experienced a cold atmosphere and the feeling of someone being there.

'Probably the weirdest experience is what happened to my beer. Three times in one lunch-time we found no beer coming through to the bar and each time it was because someone or something had turned the pressure off at the gas cylinder. Then one day, when a barrel of lager was being delivered, the gas connection on the cylinder was accidentally knocked and broken which meant we could not serve it from the bar. I had to take a couple of days off at the time and, when I returned and saw lager being served, I thought the connection had been repaired, but not a bit of it. The lager was coming up the pipes without any assistance at all! The repair man could not believe it as there was *no* way the lager could reach the bar without pressure. He got an even bigger shock when he saw the residue of lager, normally lying in the tube after drawing a pint, going back into the barrel of its own volition. He's never really liked coming here again after that.'

The Odeon Film Centre. Banging doors and unusual atmospheres.

The New Yorker Restaurant. Popular and friendly and far from 'spooky'.

There is another theory as to the identity of the spirit. Rita said she had heard it was possibly that of a workman who was killed when the cinema was originally built on the site of the old Fry's chocolate factory. Before it opened, it was said he could be heard walking behind the screen. Whoever it is, Rita says she is not afraid and any mischief is promptly dealt with by her scolding remark of 'stop messing about and go away'. In the Odeon Film Centre, Manager Mr John Lee said he and his staff have not noticed or seen anything, but admits a clairvoyant contract cleaner has experienced unusual atmospheres.

In the past I have spent many an hour at the Odeon discussing forthcoming films or attending late night previews when sometimes there was just a handful of members of the press scattered around the auditorium with a welcome whisky well after midnight. I cannot say for sure what some of us heard, but I have wondered since whether a door banging somewhere below the cinema was *really* that of an outside exit to the street.

Various kinds of phenomena can be found in presentday Bristol but an account from the past always contains those extra ingredients: the way people lived, the atmosphere enhanced by the use of candlelight. Whether we believe in the Supernatural or not, it has been around for a very long time and in 1761 the *whole* city was alive with excited talk of some very odd 'goings-on' in the Lamb Inn near Lawford's Gate.

Mr Giles, landlord of the Lamb Inn, had a large family and two of his children, Molly aged thirteen and Dobby aged eight, were tormented every night by something invisible which 'bit them on the neck and arms, and pricked them with pins; various articles of furniture being at the same time thrown about their bedroom by incomprehensible forces'. The strange disturbances brought Mr Henry Durbin to the household, a prosperous druggist of Redcliffe Street who could not give a natural explanation for the bites and scratches which appeared on the two girls as they lay in bed. Nothing happened when the girls were asleep but at other times he saw a wine glass throw itself at a nurse while 'Molly's cap flew four feet off her head, and something beat the tattoo on the bed-ticking with the skill of a drummer'. Thumping the bed, Mr Durbin heard a squeaking sound and after great deliberation concluded the experiences were the act of an evil spirit. He asked questions of the spirit designed to be answered with a series of knocks. From these he learned the phenomena had been instigated by an old witch who lived in Mangotsfield.

It was really Mr Giles the disturbances were directed against for he had started a fast carrier service of 'flying wagons' to London prompting a jealous rival to pay ten guineas to have him bewitched. Mr Giles refused to believe he was bewitched and thought it was the trickery of servants, though wagons repeatedly became stuck in the road at Hanham and needed eighteen horses to move them. Another wagon shook itself violently in the yard of the inn though no-one was near it at the time.

As the phenomena continued many members of the clergy visited the inn including those from the Cathedral and the churches of St Nicholas, St Werburgh's and Temple. They, too, questioned the spirit but in various languages and even more interestingly in thought only. All received what were considered to be truthful replies so, agreeing the spirit was evil, prayers were asked of the congregation from the pulpit. Meanwhile pins began to fly around the girls' bedroom and the girls, themselves, were thrown out of bed. No-one could hold them down as they were carried upwards to the ceiling. Major Drax, a relative of the Countess of Berkeley, a powerfully strong man, and several of his equally strong servants also found it impossible to keep the girls from rising to the ceiling. Impressed by what he saw, Major Drax took the girls to London to Court and presented them to several noblemen and bishops. It was ultimately found that the girls were only affected when kept together.

Mr Giles, meanwhile, still believed that everything was due to trickery but suddenly he was taken ill on a journey home from Bath. As he reached the place where the wagons became stuck in the road, the harness broke on his gig. He saw an old woman standing by the wheel but he felt too afraid to speak to her. He died four days later.

Despite the passing of Mr Giles, the children were still tormented and, not surprisingly by this time declined to stay at the inn. Mr Durbin again found out from the spirit that the witch had been paid more money to continue her evil work so Mrs Giles decided it was time to enlist the help of a 'white witch' known as the Cunning Woman of Bedminster. As to the remedy, it was apparently too indelicate a description to be recorded by Latimer in the *Annals of Bristol*, but it was successful. A believer in the affair stated 'scoffers of witchcraft cast a slur upon the Bible', an opinion equally held by John Wesley, yet the whole episode was still considered by some to be more simply explained. The theory given by another writer on the subject maintained it was probably due to the conniving practices of Mr Giles' mother-in-law, Mrs Nelmes who, with Mrs Giles, effected the depreciation of the inn which Mrs Nelmes eventually purchased.

Around the Churches

I love taking photographs of churches and where better than Bristol, brimming with ancient places of worship and a fascinating collection of new ones. To me they are a visual pleasure of exquisite architecture to be explored and enjoyed. In, on and around them are marvels in masonry, wood and stained glass, fashioned at a time when people, unlettered and superstitious, regarded the church as more than the

Quarter jacks on Christ Church on the corner of Broad Street — carved in 1728 by James Paty, they are a constant attraction to passers-by who pause to watch them swing and strike their bells at the quarter hour.

centre of town or village life. They were like huge story books where they could see the numerous figures of saints and holy persons and learn from their attitudes something of how to be good while less happy individuals showed them the effect of punishment.

Modern churches rise rapidly to be finished within a lifetime whereas in earlier times they took many years to build. Men, like beasts of burden, hauled great blocks of stone inspired with the religious spirit, while townsfolk watched eagerly for a part to be finished and thrilled at the sculptor's decoration. In later years additions to cathedrals were made and repairs were a matter of course. In the seventeenth century, Bristol's Christ Church spire was in need of renovation but the recording of the fact reads rather strangely. 'Christ Church spire new pointed, and an iron spear

Left: Angels and demons — guardians of faith. Gargoyles on Bristol Cathedral.
Below: Edward Blanket and his wife in St Stephen's Church off Colston Avenue. Can the legend be true that this Bristol wool merchant invented blankets?

whereon the cock standeth was set up in the old one's place, whereon was a roasting pig eaten!' During the same century hour-glasses were a common feature in churches to curb lengthy and tedious sermons.

Churches are full of curios and the curious, and today we can wander in awe around their massive structures. We can crane our necks at the pinnacles and grin at the gargoyles or we can discreetly weave among tombs, headstones and sepulchral monuments while striving to read faded script.

In the churchyard of St Luke's, Brislington is a tombstone commemorating Thomas Newman who died in 1542 at the incredible age of 153, yet its origination warrants as much speculation as the span of life. It seems that Bridlington in Yorkshire once had an identical tombstone which at some time disappeared but records show that the wording on their stone was different to the one at Brislington, so it was not stolen and brought to Bristol. It has been thought Thomas Newman was a monk who took people on

Thomas Newman's tombstone in St Luke's churchyard at Brislington.

Above: Cat's grave, St Mary Redcliffe Church. Curiosity did not kill this pussy, it gave her an ear for music! For fifteen years she lived at St Mary Redcliffe and delighted in sitting with the organist, listening while he played. The grave marks the spot where she waited each day to be let into the church.

pilgrimage from Keynsham to St Anne's Well but there is no mention of his occupation. Whoever he was, he was undoubtedly revered in two very different places and it is hard to believe he is simply a sixteenth-century joke!

From Brislington to Bath on the outskirts of the Bristol environs lies Saltford where another stone in the porch of the church commemorates a remarkable story which is undoubtedly true and certainly not meant at the time as an April Fool. It records a burial on 1 April 1723 for a lady who had yet to finish living.

Stop, Reader, and a wonder see
As strange as e'er was known;
My feet fell off from my body
In the midst of the bone.
I had no surgeon for my help,
But God Almighty's aid
On Whom I always will rely
And never be afraid.
Though here beneath interr'd they lie
Destruction for to see
Yet they shall live and reunite,
To all Eternity.

The feet were those of Frances Flood, a travelling lady from Devon who contracted an appalling case of smallpox. On the journey to Bristol she became desperately ill and took shelter in a pigstye where the strength of her faith gradually enabled her to recover despite the 'withering off' of her feet. She wrote a pamphlet of her experience and, taking to crutches, made a living by selling her story on the streets of Bristol.

Another fascinating story which aroused my curiosity for having a connection with Bristol comes from over Dundry Hill beyond Bishopsworth in the village of Chew Stoke. In the church is a chapel dedicated to St Wilgefortis, alias The Maid Uncumber, a lady of great faith and virtue. At a time unknown she was the daughter of a pagan King of Portugal but Wilgefortis was a Christian convert and, having

Left: Frances Flood's inscribed stone for her feet.

made a vow of chastity, refused to marry a man her father had chosen to be her husband. Wilgefortis prayed to God to inflict on her beautiful face some unsightly embellishment to put the suitor off. Her prayers were answered when she grew a beard and moustache but her father, more enraged than astonished, had the poor lady put to death by crucifixion. She became a popular saint with women in the Middle Ages who wished to be rid of their husbands for unhappy wives made offerings of oats to her image in the hope they would become 'uncumbered' of their husbands! Sadly the bombing in the war virtually demolished Bristol's Church of St Mary-le-Port and only the tower remains but it was here an altar dedicated to St Wilgefortis once stood for the benefit of the cumbered wives of Bristol.

Left: Chew Stoke Church. Full of angels and a chapel to St Wilgefortis.
Below: St Mary-le-Port Tower. Once there was an altar here dedicated to St Wilgefortis.

Left: St John's Gate in Broad Street — the figures of Kings Brennus and Belinus, the legendary founders of Bristol in 390 BC, watch over the only remaining gateway through the once old walled city.

Above: Clifton Cathedral — the Roman Catholic Cathedral of St Peter and St Paul — a creation in concrete. Its three rising members form curious combinations when viewed from different parts of the city.

One curiosity can lead to another for Chew Stoke Church could be called the Church of Angels, 156 of them to be exact. One of them over a window in the south aisle is missing, removed by a displeased rector because its face resembled that of the Devil. The tale goes that when the church was refurbished in the 1860s, the building contractor delayed paying the wages, prompting the mason to depict what he thought of his employer in the features of the face.

Churches can be as full of surprising stories as they are of treasures. Tragically many beautiful things disappeared in a holocaust of desecration during the Civil War, an event which caused much protest and persecution. Yet curiously during the Reformation the people of the church meekly stripped their places of worship to suit the mood of the day. Altars and other items of decoration were carried out under one monarch and calmly replaced under another. We can recall the days of pre-Christianity in what remain of the curious symbols of pagan belief in fertility, mythical creatures and the demons from the shadows of hell. Yet churches are places of tranquillity, of spiritual refreshment and artistic beauty, an escape from the surrounding confusion of city and suburban streets. They are also symbols of faith, the curious something we find hard to understand, the most hot-blooded of all passionate things and the most powerful. They will continue to be huge story books, turning the pages in history and reflecting the changes in our way of life. As I wander around them, like others I feel encouraged to move quietly to speak in soft tones. Like faith itself, churches will always leave a lasting, mysterious impression.

Right: Westbury-on-Trym churchyard. A fascinating quiet corner.

The Streets of Bristol

Although I 'gnash' my teeth at large and overpowering modern village name-signs to be seen around Bristol's outer suburbs, for they kill any charm of approach, I cheer the reinstatement in the city of the Three Lamps signpost at the junction of the Bath and Wells roads at Totterdown. It points its pretty nineteenth-century way in open 'Egyptian' lettering against the sky. On the column is the Roman numeral III which refers to the popular belief of three lamps once lighting the three roads. Further down the Bath Road is the curious name — Thunderbolt Steps.

Right: The Three Lamps Signpost: 'It points its pretty nineteeth-century way . . .'
Below: Bristol Bridge in 1830 complete with 'kiosk' style shops.

The streets signs of Bristol make fascinating reading. I have often wondered about the origins of unusual names which by their description promote fanciful ideas of past traditions, or stranger habits and happenings. It seems street names were absent until 1791 for very few people were able to read. During the early years of the century more conspicuous signs could be seen for the identification of trades and Latimer's *Annals of Bristol* describes the scene vividly. He tells '. . . of the curious medley of figures which sought to catch the eye of spectators. Lions, spread-eagles, griffins, elephants and tigers were to be seen of every tint. Suns, moons, and stars were equally popular. Wheat-sheaves, bee-hives, horses, blackbirds, grasshoppers, dogs, hares . . . A great number of tradesmen flaunted a double device, such as the Tye Wig and Griffin of a barber; the Hand and Pen of a schoolmaster; the Half Moon and Wheat-sheaf of a draper; and the Sword and Crown of a cutler. Booksellers frequently adopted the Bible and Sun; and at least one undertaker set up the lugubrious representation of a Coffin and Shroud. Even the business of the stamp office was conducted "at the sign of the King's Arms". Wood carvers and painters must have reaped a good harvest in carrying out the eccentric conceptions of their patrons, for it appears that some of the signs cost from £20 to £40 each. Whatever may have been the artistic results of their labours, the swinging designs, which from morn till eve threw moving shadows over the pavement, must have presented a quaint attractiveness and variety now entirely lost.'

Many street names commemorate famous people but who was King Dick? In the parish of St George, King Dick's Lane is a reminder of a sailor who fought at the Battle of Trafalgar. He retired to the district and, a colourful character, he was often seen proudly carrying his telescope like Lord Nelson under his arm while he paraded the streets. His manner earned him from the locals the name we see officially displayed today.

Other names evolve from the simple art of direction, the constant use of obvious landmarks, pubs, trades or even trees. Wild Country Lane at Long Ashton retains its description but not far away is puzzling Lovelinch Gardens. Granny's Lane between Kingswood and Hanham conjures up childhood memories but I wonder who's

Right: Robin Hood Lane: '. . . a curious idea for its origin.'

granny it was who lived there? Back in St George in the Redfield district, the curious past presents itself in George and Dragon Lane. We can easily assume the inn of the same name beside the lane can take credit for this one but we cannot be sure it was not used before the inn was built. The area of St George dates from ancient times when Clouds Hill was called a 'clud', a mass of rock, and the cult of St George was still fresh in the minds of people. Sadly the lane is now almost non-existent submerged in modern development.

Off Lewins Mead is Johnny Ball Lane, once called Bartholomews Lane. It appears the change was due to one John a Ball who was thought to have been involved in the building of Bristol Bridge. He was certainly the owner of property which stood near the once Franciscan Friary in Lewins Mead. Not far from Christmas Steps is Zed Alley, so called because of its winding nature, but I must admit it looks pretty straight to me.

Another legend lives on in narrow Robin Hood Lane off St Michael's Hill. Although a reminder of the gallant champion of the poor from farther afield, there is a curious idea for its origin given by E.F. Wells in his *Egypt in Bristol* where he suggests it is derived from *Ra-benu* or the Rising Sun. He draws on the strange theory of Alfred

Left: Pitch and Pay Lane, The Downs. To prevent the spread of plague in the seventeenth century, people from the city threw their money over a barrier to countryfolk who in return threw their goods back.

Below: Catbrain Lane, Henbury. The name is derived from the Old English 'Cates-brazen' meaning rough clay mixed with stones. More curiously, the name has been attributed to shapes of fossils found in the old quarry. Although seemingly quiet, it is surrounded by acres of modern-day development.

Westbury-on-Trym. Another cheerfully pointing signpost.

Watkins who discovered the enigmatic ley lines of power which are said to cross our countryside and quotes from his *Old Straight Track*. 'The number of Robin Hood's Butts and hills and earthworks absolutely disprove the idea that the origin of this name was an outlaw of the Middle Ages. The name was assuredly much earlier.' Wells' own conclusion was to see the situation of the lane as being 'not unlikely to have been a place where the rising sun was worshipped. The hill commands wide views to the south and west and the lane actually faces east.' If the theory is true it is thought-provoking, for we can see the Robin Hood public house on the corner of the lane as The Rising Sun – an appropriate name for many an inn.

Coming back to earth there is World's End Lane, obviously named for it slopes to nowhere, and practical thoughts surround Old Broad Street, Cheese Lane and Chiphouse Road. We can wonder about living in Hot Water Lane while envying those in Lucky Lane but what about Thunderbolt Steps, winding steeply up to Totterdown from the Bath Road. Was the hillside once struck by a thunderbolt? Some people call them Thunder and Lightning Steps and one can imagine viewing from the top a storm over the city, while a slip on the way down could promote a descent more like greased lightning.

Like London, Bristol has its Petticoat Lane and Constitution Hill and like many places it has its Broad Street and High Street, but I doubt anywhere else can equal the historical grandeur of cobbled King Street and Corn Street with its nails. I can understand Latimer's feelings over the loss of the swinging signs of the eighteenth century. What a grand sight they must have been: a far cry from today's curious planning requirements where a clinical appearance and consideration for the 'sporadic view' is cluttered by road traffic signs and yellow plastic rubbish bins while special permission is required to fly the Union Jack. In political mood I can traverse Meg Thatcher's Green in St George or enjoy climbing Brandon Hill without a carpet, where an ancient notice warns of 'kicking up the dust': 'No carpet beating allowed before 6 am or after 9 pm'.

Curious Corners

Right: On the corner of Hope Chapel Hill and Granby Hill. Barred from the steps to the door!

Below: A multifarious collection of memorabilia in a corner of Clifton Antiques Market. Military medals and pastel-coloured chubby china bunnies join pictures and postcards, tools and trinkets and other intriguing things.

Few chemists display such a sign and fewer such delightful window displays. Closer inspection will reveal the strange shapes of old bottles and the elegant glass symbols of the apothecary with their liquids of bright ruby red and golden hues.

Right: Down in the city, my favourite curious corner — Leonard Lane. Lit by gas, the lamps light the narrow way inside the boundary of the old city wall. Behind the closed doors and assorted styles of façade and graffiti, all manner of business ensues including a chocolate factory.

Some Curious Cures

Actius doth say: 'The soles of the Feet anointed with the fat of the Dormouse doth procure sleep.' On reflection I will stick to my hop pillow. Some of the cures for ailments in earlier centuries were certainly ludicrous not to mention repulsive and in the main were a legacy from the ancient past based on superstition and a form of faith.

In Bristol the glorified Hotwell was considered far from desirable for some patients suffered 'dirt, stench, chilling blasts and perpetual rains', yet still people flocked believing the dirty waters would cure anything. Although the use of mud is still popular, at some spas in the country the patient might be forgiven for feeling little hope as he or she was led to a coffin-shaped casket to be covered by mud and left to wallow. Rheumatism, paralysis and nervous disorders were said to have been helped by a dip in the Cold Bath at Castle Ditch until it fell down into the Avon in 1772 along with part of the wall of St Peter's Hospital. During the same century, the waters of the Avon receded for so long that well water became undrinkable, foul smelling and discoloured and the Hotwell ran red as blood. Belief in the waters as a cure became overshadowed by fear as everyone rushed to the churches thinking 'the end was nigh'. Confidence soon returned when the phenomenon was thought to be caused by an earthquake in Lisbon!

A visit to the doctor in earlier centuries was a hazardous occupation. There was once the widespread belief that toothache was caused by a worm and a variety of herbs, acorns and even wax was used to treat the tooth in the hope the worm would die and drop out. Worm or no worm, perhaps it was more effective than we know for even today nutmeg is known to help pain before the dreaded visit. The value of herbs is recognised in modern treatments for many things, but I think Culpeper went a bit too far when he offered the following cure for gout: 'Take an owl, pull of her feathers, and pull out her guts;

The Rising Sun at Castle Ditch in the eighteenth century. A more welcome cure than a cold bath!

salt her well for a week, then put her into a pot, and stop it close, and put her into an oven, that so she may be brought into a mummy, which beat into powder and mixed with boar's grease, is an excellent remedy.'

We say 'boo' to a hiccup sufferer and drop cold keys down backs for nosebleeds but fright was considered a marvellous cure for ague. Horrifying stories were manufactured to put sufferers in a 'tizzy'. While they believed in some terrible dilemma, the fever was 'worked' out of the system. Old cures are still used for rheumatism such as the wearing of copper bracelets and I even knew someone who carried the right fore-foot of a female hare in their pocket. It is still possible to find someone to charm away warts but another idea was to pull a hair from the scalp, tie as many knots in it as there are warts, then throw it away. For whooping cough the good news is to ride a piebald horse but if it does not work, try the bad news. Find a spider and the bigger the better. Hold it over the head and say:

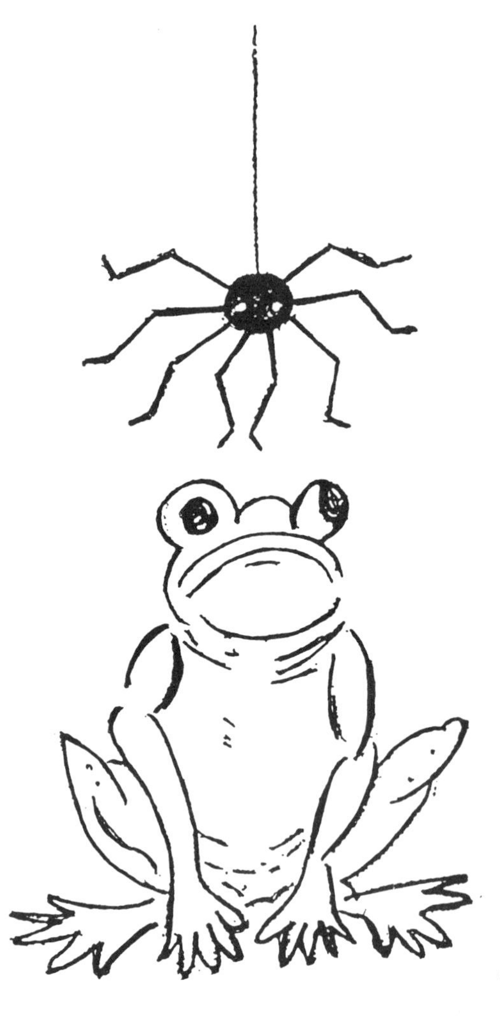

'Take one large spider, large frog or toad . . .'

Spider, as you waste away,
Whooping cough no longer stay.

Then hang it over the mantelpiece until it is all dried up.

A touch of 'eye of newt' seems to lie beneath the use of toads or frogs for many disorders in the past. One large fat toad baked dry then ground to powder and used like snuff was another cure for nosebleeds but equal confidence was placed in the use of prayer as illustrated by this rhyme for severe burns:

There were two angels came from the north,
One brought fire, the other brought frost;
Come out fire, go in frost,
Father Son and Holy Ghost.

It seems that faith was an important qualification for a physician looking for a position in the eighteenth century. For the non-British applicant an advertisement in 1778 stresses: 'No objection to a Jew Doctor, provided he professes to believe in Christianity and attends Divine Service on all Charity Sermon Days.'

There is no doubt that in past ages medicine included superstitious practice, charms, incantation and all manner of nonsense. Yet we cannot ignore the wonders performed by surgery in those days, for even some of those early instruments are still in use today. There is also much to be learned by modern medics as to how herbs were used to advantage in the past. While we still search for the elusive cure for the common cold, perhaps there is more to gain from nature's own store and her creatures, like the snake with its venom. But can the froth from a snail cure earache? I have my reservations just as I have about prescribing the following as an answer to the dreams of balding men: 'It is said that Mice dung, with the Ashes of burned Wasps, and Hazel Nuts, and a little Vinegar of Roses put thereto, doth trimly deck a bald Place with Hairs if the same Place be often rubbed or anointed therewith.' Anyone care to give it a try?

Follies

Ornamental Gothic towers and sham castles, the eye-catching follies of Bristol were built with the funds of the wealthy and add a frivolous charm to the landscape. Conceived with a degree of make-believe mixed with fierce pride, they stand in the main as memorials to successful men who were far from foolish. Unfortunately their self-indulgence brought some derision in the eighteenth century and often they were considered eccentric. A poem of 1746 criticises two 'useless' follies long since gone from either side of the Avon Gorge:

Let Cook and Norton tow'ring Follies raise,
They wisdome, Wallis, will I sing and praise;
Let heroes and Prime Ministers of State
Smile when they're called ironically, great;
Superior merit shall my muse employ,
Since better 'tis to save than to destroy.

The wisdom of public benefactor John Wallis was to build a safety wall high above the River Avon on the edge of the Downs and along to the boundary of Sneyd Park. Wallis's Wall, as it was called, greatly reduced the risk of fatal accidents but strangely such a man is no longer immediately remembered for today we know it as Sea Walls.

Follies can be fun, fantasies to feed the imagination as their builders intended. Children play out their dreams around the Sham Castle on the Blaise Castle estate at Henbury which Thomas Farr built in 1766. His dream of it being fit for habitation was never fulfilled but it has remained a tourist attraction for 200 years and

Right: The sham castle on the Blaise estate, where 'children play out their dreams'.

always a popular place of recreation for the public. The Observatory, looking over the Gorge and the Suspension Bridge, attracts thousands to its camera obscura. Once a snuff mill which burnt down during a terrific gale in 1777, William West converted it in 1828 so that curious eyes could see through telescopes 'a magical effect. The movement of persons, animals and carriages, the waving of foliage and the coming and going of ships being brought into the picture with distinction and vivid colouring of nature and affording a high gratification to the observer from the continual changes, varying effects of light and shade upon the landscape.' It still holds a magic today.

Probably the most beautiful folly in the country is Clifton's Goldney House Grotto and gardens owned by Bristol University.

Goldney House Tower and Grotto. 'Where lingering drops from mineral roofs distil.'

The twelve-acre gardens contain a Gothic summer-house and terrace with a Gothic tower holding the supply of water which falls to the grotto below. William Heard wrote of Thomas Goldney's creation in 1778:

Deep in the rock his coolly grotto *lies,*
Of splendid stones, where brilliant pillars rise;
Where every shell, of every glowing hue,
In elegant composure charm the view:
'Where lingering drops from mineral roofs distil,
'And pointed crystals, break the sparkling rill;
'Unpolished gems no ray on pride bestow,
'And latent metals innocently glow'

In complete contrast down in the city behind Temple Meads is St Vincent's Works in Silverthorne Lane. Set in an area of industrial

St Vincent's Works. 'Not generally regarded as a folly.'

fervour, its neo-Norman 'castle' style is a light relief. It is not generally regarded as a folly for it was designed by Thomas Royce Lysaght for his industrialist brother John and housed the offices of a thriving iron galvanizing plant. It can be argued that the works were built for a useful purpose but it is an example of the inconsistency surrounding the curious definition of the word 'folly'. The embattled frontage of this fairy-tale fantasy cannot escape its inclusion in this chapter.

The Quaker, William Reeve, created in Brislington in the 1760s, his house called Mount Pleasant, known today as Arnos Court Hotel containing Reeves Nightclub. As one of the 'big spenders', he built on the other side of the road his Black Castle, now a public house, which housed his stables and servants' quarters. Its walls, dramatically constructed from black copper-slag blocks from his own Crew's Hole brass founding works, must have been an imposing sight in the eighteenth century. 'The dirtiest great shop I ever saw,' said Horace Walpole when visiting Bristol in 1766. He thought it was the Devil's Cathedral. Reeve did not stop there either. He also built a colonnaded cold Bath House with dressing rooms and a pinery, then constructed a tunnel under the road connecting it to the Court and the Castle. He acquired a gateway from Bristol and four medieval statues for embellishment, rebuilt it near the Black Castle and named it Arnos Gateway. Then he went bankrupt. The complex of buildings was a folly in the sense of the word and the Quaker Society of Friends were none too pleased. They considered Reeve's dilemma had been brought on himself through a lack of religious principle and overspending, so he was expelled from the fraternity.

In the 1950s a little bit of Brislington was destined to go to Wales. The Bath House had lain derelict for years, its former glory neglected and crumbling. Tudor Edwards in his book *Bristol* wrote of a 'principal building . . . isolated in the middle of cabbage patches and December roses, its Gothic details thinly disguising an essentially classical building topped with urns and having gazebo-like pavilions at the sides . . . the octagonal bath having a coved ceiling and cornice of elaborate plasterwork now badly mutilated . . . Its former refinements are yet discernible in the garlands and human heads and in one intact panel modelled with what was probably intended to be a castle on the banks of the Arno in Italy.' No wonder Welsh architect Sir Clough Williams-Ellis considered the colonnaded building a curiosity worth acquiring when the decision for demolition came in

Left: The Black Castle. 'The dirtiest great shop I ever saw.'
Right: Arnos Court. Not so salubrious today and its Bath House gone.

1957. He planned to place it amid his collection of architectural styles in his extraordinary Italianate village of Portmeirion. Moving the building to its romantic setting in North Wales is graphically described by Sir Clough Williams-Ellis in his book *Portmeirion.*

'The transporting of some hundred tons of fragile and elaborately wrought masonry two hundred miles by road was no light matter, but it was as nothing to the feat of delicate dismembering at the sending end or of the faultless re-assembly of the jigsaw at this. At Bristol a devoted architect made a precise measured survey for me showing every single stone, each numbered on the drawing as well as on itself, and an equally skilled and co-operative builder, expert in church restorations, undertook the tricky stone-by-stone demolition.

'I confess that I was myself not a little daunted by the complexity of the diagrams and lists and sequence schedules that we had to work from as well as by the confused scatteration of architectural debris that littered half the car park. But not so my master mason, Mr William Davies. He imperturbably took over all the papers along with the intimidating stoneheaps and methodically set about their

The Colonnade in the Italianate village of Portmeirion.

resurrection into what now presides so becomingly over the upper lawn.'

A 'glory' which was lost to Bristol rose again for its new owner in an honoured situation and, as he said, 'having determined its site and fixed its levels, there was little more for me to do but look on, approve, and very much admire'. Among 'the various pavilions and such that punctuate the light verse of Portmeirion's peculiar saga', the Colonnade can be seen today in the lovely coastal village of the 'land of song'. Although the Bath House was not reconstructed, its Main Staircase window and a doorway were incorporated in other buildings in the village.

Curious Customs from the Past

Local fairs and festivals have become customary events and a popular source of public entertainment in Bristol each year.

People gather to watch the May Day Morris dancing on Castle Green when a day-long tour of the Almshouses is made or to see the colourful civic occasions with the Lord Mayor's coach and horses. At one time public occasions were virtually the only communal entertainment people had.

In the eighteenth century cock-fighting and bear-baiting were common and there was the customary duck hunting in a pool which now lies under Bathurst Basin. The thrill of catching your duck was usually followed by a parade of the city bounds, an occasion of great excitement, drawing large numbers of followers. Anyone thought to be too high-spirited would find themselves grabbed and bumped against the boundary stones with a sore result, yet still considered to be part of the day's fun.

Bristol was rich in Mummers' plays and even in the early twentieth century, groups of six or more men could be seen dancing in the streets of Stapleton and Bedminster adorned in sacks and bells singing words on a theme of 'Jack the Ripper'. In medieval times apprentices and young labourers were favoured with holidays on Shrove Tuesday. May Day was the best holiday of all when folk flocked to Durdham Down decked with stalls and an opportunity for games. In the morning, greetings were sung from the top of St Stephen's tower and throughout the day the colourful figure of Jack-in-the-Green dressed in ribbons and streamers could be seen in the Horsefair.

The need for entertainment encouraged large gatherings at public hangings, resulting in an unsavoury curiosity, while the funerals of the wealthy provided a spectacular parade. Sometimes at the cost of exhausting the estate, the deceased would have left instructions for a

London
Coffee House
1713
TEA BLENDERS
CARWARDINES
ROASTERS

Above: The Horsefair in 1880 where once was seen the colourful figure of Jack-in-the-Green. Left: Carwardines coffee shop, The London Coffee House, in Corn Street. Once '. . . full of seditious secretaries and disloyal persons.'

funeral 'to be remembered' and to which all of importance were invited. Bells tolled for long hours, the dirge being heard all over Bristol. Costly presents were given of clothes to chosen members of the poor and gold rings for the mourners. Usually at midnight, the cortège, flamboyant with 'escutcheons, sconces, waxlights, flambeaux, plumes, pennons and mutes' would wend its way through the streets to the church. Such a sight was at times too tempting for an irreverent thief who from the darkness would snatch at velvet drapings or ornaments. After the funeral would come the 'wake' where the many guests feasted on a costly assortment of funeral meats and a large amount of liquor. In Kingswood it was not uncommon for liquor to help to 'lighten the load' at less important funerals when four strong men would carry the coffin from pub to pub on the way to the church.

On the wall of Carwardine's coffee shop in Corn Street, we can read the words 'the liquifaction of our torrefaction ensures satisfaction' and the tempting aroma of roasting coffee beans assures us it will. Yet, when the building was the site of the London Coffee House in the seventeenth century, the custom of taking coffee was much more of an institution. The London Coffee House was one of many such places in Bristol where not only coffee was consumed but also large quantities of ale, cider or Bristol Milk, accompanied by a lavish selection of food. Merchants transacted their business amid the bustle of what was virtually a house of entertainment, a veritable 'speakers' corner' where all kinds of people congregated in an atmosphere thick with smoke.

Curious for news, the main interest for customers would be the arrival of newsletters and papers from London, the political content of which was generally a matter for fervent debate. Inevitably free speech gave cause for concern among local officials and those of an established mind. Coffee houses were viewed with suspicion and considered a 'hot bed' of bad influences, places full of 'seditious secretaries and disloyal persons'. Gradually in the eighteenth century the custom declined but not before the Reverend William Goldwin, Master of the Bristol Grammar School, wrote in his *Poetical Description of Bristol*:

Here wise Remarkers on the Church and State
O'er Turkish Lap and smoaky Whiffs debate.
Here half shut Authors in Confusion lye
And kindling Stuffs for Party Heats supply.

It is interesting if not curious to note how little people have changed over the past 300 years. Customary habits still remain in a tempered society. 'Let's meet for coffee' we say today and relish the chance to meet an old friend, catch up on some news, even discuss business in a premises no longer considered a 'den of sin and iniquity'. We still go duck hunting and some funerals have a 'wake' and we certainly have our share of felons and foul deeds. If we are honest, even without a hanging, we may see the fever for revenge in a watcher who searches for the face under the blanket.

There is one custom in law which added profound weight to the old saying of 'not in front of the ladies'. Some of us may have a 'swear-box' but how about a revival from the past where the anonymous reporting to the Magistrate of 'profane cursing or swearing' was liable to a hefty fine? We can well imagine the rich 'pickings' for today's Corporation coffers.

SS Great Britain – a Living Legend

Some say ships lost their romance with the passing of sail, but Bristol's unique maritime heritage ensures that, here at least, this romance will never die.

I shall never forget the day the *Great Britain*, her hull covered with barnacles from colder climes, eased her way up the River Avon. There was a potent atmosphere as welcoming cheers from the crowded river bank and Clifton Suspension Bridge above, resounded in the Gorge. What a birthday I had the next day as I feasted my eyes on the marvel of engineering which had returned to the heart of fine British ship building.

Curiously, it all began with the ill health of the great engineer Isambard Kingdom Brunel. Convalescing in Bristol with a broken leg

Launch of "The Great Britain" Steamship at Bristol July 19th. 1843.

left Brunel's mind in a fervour of activity, dreaming of achievement, for he was no ordinary man. A talented and precocious child, by the age of six he could draw well and master the principles of geometry. Maturity saw his genius fired by competition and a temperament which gave the relatively little man the reputation of a 'workaholic' and 'slave-driver'. Privately he admitted to 'self conceit and a love of glory' but it was this spirit of determination and conviction which matched the spirit of Bristol. Brunel forged his way through the city using energy and vision: Clifton Suspension Bridge, the city docks, the railway and his first ship the *Great Western*, which gave him the

The launching of the *Great Eastern* steamship with Brunel second from right.

On board the *Great Britain* at San Francisco in 1885. Note the chickens.
Overleaf: Another of Brunel's achievements — the Clifton Suspension Bridge.

confidence for his concept for the *Great Britain.* Perhaps only Brunel would have accepted with complacency a prophecy of the ship's long and illustrious destiny.

The *Great Britain* 'floated out' of her dry dock on 19 July 1843 in the presence of the Prince Consort, Prince Albert. As a declared holiday, thousands lined the waterside cheering, while church bells pealed and cannon boomed. After returning to the building dock for fitting out and having the engines installed, she sailed out again the following year to begin her life in service with an enthusiastic welcome in every port.

Brunel had triumphed with the Atlantic liner and so had Bristol. She was the first iron ship driven by propeller, an unrivalled pioneer of the seas with the luxurious comforts for passengers befitting a Victorian age.

She was to spend 31 years passenger carrying followed by ten years with cargo before the raging seas around Cape Horn dictated that her sailing days were over. Laden with coal and leaking, she was forced to limp to the Falkland Islands for shelter, arriving in Port Stanley on 26 May 1886. The Falkland Islands Company soon recognised her value as a floating storage vessel and so began an incredible 51 years of housing coal and wool. The *Great Britain's* usefulness came to an end in 1937 and she was towed a few miles away to Sparrow Cove to be beached and abandoned.

Against a seemingly barren and stark landscape with its rocky inlets, the *Great Britain* lay in a part of the world that knows the cruelty of vicious gales, driving snow and mountainous seas. Left at the mercy of the elements to rot, she settled in icy waters and lay silently listening to the call of the geese. As the years passed she became rooted in the landscape, a home for seabirds and marine life. She was a familiar landmark to sailors while earning a special place in the hearts of the Islanders. Although a shell with her former glory gone, she retained a

Left: The SS *Great Britain* in full sail.
Right: and Below: On her way home to Bristol.

The *Great Britain* is towed up the River Avon to welcoming cheers.

majestic quality. With masts held high, she proudly displayed the fine lines of her unique bows, designed for speed. As she lay in the southern regions of the globe, echoes from the past began to revive memories of her magnificence in earlier days.

Across the Atlantic, stirrings began in the 1950s at the Maritime Museum in San Francisco with thoughts of a salvaging and restoration operation. In England, a naval architect, Ewan Corlett, became interested in the *Great Britain's* history and wrote to *The Times* urging the authorities to 'do something to recover the ship and place her on display'. In 1968 meetings were held in London and Bristol to discuss the practicalities of a British salvage expedition, which caused the Americans to politely withdraw and concede to a British claim.

Nearly home as she passes through the Cumberland Basin Bridge.

The 'SS *Great Britain* Project' was formed with Richard Goold-Adams as Chairman, and a visit to the Falklands by Ewan Corlett with the help of the Admiralty confirmed recovery was possible. Spirits were high equalling the earlier energy and vision of Brunel. Support grew with the encouragement of Prince Philip. Funds began to trickle through until a generous boost came from Jack Hayward, the Bahamas-based British philanthropist. Finally the Islanders agreed to let a much loved possession go.

In 1970 the *Great Britain* woke from her 33 years of slumbers, surrounded by a hive of activity. While being lifted, she cooperated, as forecast by Ewan Corlett, by closing a crack and straightening her twist. She rose from the water on the submersible pontoon *Mulus III* and was taken to Port Stanley for securing. 24 April saw the ship with masts removed heading for home, towed by the tug *Varius II* and her Anglo-German salvage crew. Off the Welsh coast Bristol tugs took over and on 23 June she arrived in Avonmouth on the pontoon to a resounding welcoming 'hoot' from every ship in port.

Bristol went 'wild' on 5 July 1970. A hundred thousand people watched from the waterside as the *Great Britain*, floating on her own bottom, was triumphantly towed up the River Avon to Bristol. After waiting for a high spring tide, she was guided carefully through the shallow and narrow entrance to the Great Western drydock where she is seen today. The pull of the spirit of Bristol had completed its work — the 'Queen' was home.

Call it coincidence or what you will but I have my own theories about certain circumstances which surrounded the *Great Britain's* homecoming, her first and only return to Bristol after exactly 127 years. The high spring tide for her berthing in the drydock took place on 19 July. Strangely, this was the anniversary of her first plates being laid there on 19 July 1839 *and* of her launch there on 19 July 1843. Also, the Sunday evening of the convenient spring tide on 19 July proved to be the only possible time when the Duke of Edinburgh could be present at short notice for her redocking. We can remember here too that Prince Albert, the Prince Consort, had launched her. Another interesting facet is one which had an important bearing on the future of the *Great Britain*. During the period when the ship was being salvaged, economic developments in Bristol had led to the closing of Bristol City Docks to ordinary commerical traffic. So the decision to bring the *Great Britain* home was a momentous one for the City Council, received with deep gratitude by the Project and applauded by the people of Bristol. Mysteriously everything fitted into place as though it was intended.

I have followed the gradual changes in the ship's appearance and admired the results of restoration from the dedicated labours of Project members. I also see the many visitors who crowd her deck in the summer, curious to see the ship which in her day was revolutionary and set new standards for all later ship building. I have to believe the return of the *Great Britain* to Bristol was as predestined as was her creation. I also believe the spirit of Bristol is very much alive as the City and her ship strive to maintain a heritage — she is truly a living legend.

ALSO AVAILABLE

UNKNOWN BRISTOL

by Rosemary Clinch.

Introduced by David Foot, this is Bossiney's first Bristol title. 'Rosemary Clinch relishes looking round the corners and under the pavement stones . . .'

'Not a normal guide . . . it's a lovely book and very interesting . . .'

Penny Downs, BBC Radio Bristol

SUPERNATURAL IN SOMERSET

by Rosemary Clinch.

Atmospheres, healing, dowsing, fork-bending and strange encounters are only some of the subjects featured inside these pages. A book, destined to entertain and enlighten — one which will trigger discussion — certain to be applauded and attacked.

'. . . an illustrated study of strange encounters and extraordinary powers . . .'

Somerset County Gazette

UNKNOWN SOMERSET

by Rosemary Clinch and Michael Williams.

A journey across Somerset, visiting off-the-beaten-track places of interest. Many specially commissioned photographs by Julia Davey add to the spirit of adventure.

'Magical Somerset . . . from ley lines to fork-bending; a journey into the unknown. . . a guide which makes an Ordnance Survey map "an investment in adventure".'

Western Daily Press

100 YEARS IN SOMERSET

by Monica Wyatt.

Spans the century in words and pictures.

'This is a lovely book. As you browse through the pages every picture seems to catch your eye and sends you off on a different track.'

Polly Lloyd, BBC Radio Bristol

PEOPLE & PLACES IN BRISTOL

Introduced by E.V. Thompson.

Five authors take a look at People & Places in Bristol: E.V. Thompson, David Foot, Jillian Powell, Jack Russell and Rosemary Clinch.

'Words and pictures — many of them especially commissioned for this book — portray a rich Bristol heritage.'

West Review

OFFBEAT SOMERSET

by Dan Lees.

Author and journalist, Dan Lees, explores some off-beat stories and characters of Somerset.

'. . . he has looked at the story behind the story . . .'

Somerset & Avon Life

MYSTERIES IN THE SOMERSET LANDSCAPE
by Sally Jones.
Sally Jones, in her fourth Bossiney title, travels among the Mysteries in the Somerset Landscape. An intriguing journey among deep mysteries in a 'fascinating and varied landscape.'
'This is a whirlwind package holiday of sorcery and legend, touching down here and there before whizzing off in search of still more fascinating fare.'
Mid Somerset Series of Newspapers

LEGENDS OF SOMERSET
by Sally Jones. 65 photographs and drawings.
Sally Jones travels across rich legendary landscapes. Words, drawings and photographs all combine to evoke a spirit of adventure.
'On the misty lands of the Somerset plain — as Sally Jones makes clear — history, legend and fantasy are inextricably mixed.'
Dan Lees, The Western Daily Press

E.V. THOMPSON'S WESTCOUNTRY
This is a memorable journey: combination of colour and black-and-white photography. Bristol to Land's End happens to be the Bossiney region, and this is precisely E.V. Thompson's Westcountry.
'Stunning photographs and fascinating facts make this an ideal book for South West tourists and residents alike — beautifully atmospheric colour shots make browsing through the pages a real delight.'
Jane Leigh, Express & Echo

PARANORMAL IN THE WESTCOUNTRY
by Michael Williams.
'Michael Williams of Bossiney Books has produced another of his well illustrated books of strange goings-on . . . He explores ghost hunting, healing, psychic painting, tarot cards, mediumship, psycho-expansion, astrology and more.'
Allan Tudor, Herald Express

GHOSTS OF SOMERSET
by Peter Underwood.
The President of the Ghost Club completes a hat-trick of hauntings for Bossiney.
'. . . ghostly encounters that together make up the rich tapestry of the Ghosts of Somerset.'
Western Gazette

We shall be pleased to send you our catalogue giving full details of our growing list of titles for Devon, Cornwall and Somerset and forthcoming publications.

If you have difficulty in obtaining our titles, write direct to Bossiney Books, Land's End, St Teath, Bodmin, Cornwall.